GRATEFUL DEAD®
Built to Last

25th ANNIVERSARY ALBUM
1965 - 1990

Jamie Jensen

A PLUME BOOK

PLUME
Published by the Penguin Group
Penguin Books USA Inc., 375 Hudson Street, New York, New York 10014, U.S.A.
Penguin Books Ltd, 27 Wrights Lane, London W8 5TZ, England
Penguin Books Australia Ltd, Ringwood, Victoria, Australia
Penguin Books Canada Ltd, 2801 John Street, Markham, Ontario, Canada L3R 1B4
Penguin Books (N.Z.) Ltd, 182-190 Wairau Road, Auckland 10, New Zealand

Penguin Books Ltd, Registered Offices: Harmondsworth, Middlesex, England

Published by Plume, an imprint of New American Library, a division of Penguin Books
USA Inc. Published in England by Fantail Publishing, an imprint of Puffin Enterprises,
a division of Penguin Books Ltd.

First Plume Printing, November, 1990
10 9 8 7 6 5 4 3 2 1

Permission to reproduce printed text from the following sources is gratefully acknowledged:

Playing in the Band: An Oral and Visual Portrait of the Grateful Dead, by David Gans.
Copyright © by David Gans. Reprinted by permission of St. Martin's Press, Inc.

The Music Never Stopped, by Blair Jackson. Copyright © 1983 by Blair Jackson.

Countless issues of *Golden Road* copyright © Blair Jackson.

Deadbase III: The Complete Guide to Grateful Dead Song Lists, by John W. Scott, Stuart
Nixon, and Michael Dolgushkin. Copyright © 1989 by John W. Scott, Stuart Nixon, and
Michael Dolgushkin.

Storming Heaven: LSD and the American Dream, by Jay Stevens. Copyright © 1987 by Jay
Stevens. Reprinted by permission of the Atlantic Monthly Press.

The Electric Kool-Aid Acid Test, by Tom Wolfe. Copyright © 1968 by Tom Wolfe. Reprinted
by permission of Farrar, Straus & Giroux.

All lyrics quoted herein copyright © Ice Nine Publishing, 1990.

Thanks to Dennis McNally from the Grateful Dead.

Many thanks to everyone in the Grateful Dead organization, especially Eileen Law, Kidd
Candelario, Dan Healy and Danny Rifkin, and to Jude Heller at Lucasfilm. For help along
the way, thanks also to Jerilyn Brandelius, David Gans, Rosie McGee Ende, Jim Marshall,
Bill Smythe, the Rough Guides crew, and Wanda Whiteley at Fantail. On the home front,
love to Catherine, Brando and Judah.

Library of Congress Catalogue Card Number: 90-063008

Printed in the United States of America
Text written and photographs compiled by Jamie Jensen
Designed by Dave Crook

Contents

"All the years combine, they melt into a dream"

Bill Smythe

"All of my friends came to see me last night"

Bill Smythe

"You know it's gonna get stranger, so let's get on with the show..."

Bill Smythe

In memory of a brother
BRENT MYDLAND
1952 - 1990

Dear Deadheads, Bozos, Bolos & Assorted Intrepid Incorrigibles,

As we wallow toward the climax of our first quarter century as a traveling circus and atomic jukebox, it's gratifying to see other representatives of the grizzled old guard tuning up and hitting the road again. As the 1990s get rolling, the perception that this is an oddity will give way to the realization that Rock & Roll is not only a game for beginners.. but a plausible lifetime's work, given good will between audiences and performers determined to weather the decades without abandoning the vivid sense of ongoing community living music dispenses. This, for us, is the only certain message of the bewildering 80s.

Dying young or burning out no longer appears the only alternative for the perpetrators of Rock, a turn of events which never occurred to the caustic critics of our haphazard beginnings... maybe not even to ourselves.

As long as your interest provides momentum, we'll travel with you toward a destination whose true nature is anybody's guess. Some have pointed out that we've already arrived but that only shows the nature of the yardstick they use to reckon by. Nobody's finished.. we ain't hardly begun.

Grateful Dead and Family

INTRODUCTION

Bill Smythe

Bill Smythe

Bill Smythe

Bill Smythe

Listening to someone explain what's so great about the Grateful Dead can be a bit like having them tell you about this wild dream they had last night. Everything about the band is described with passionate intensity, and though there are lots of captivating bits and pieces that seem to be leading somewhere, things never quite hold together, never quite seem to make sense. That's because, like a dream, what's special about the band can only really be 'got' by experience, by seeing for yourself the unique event that is the Grateful Dead in concert.

It's often said there's nothing like a Grateful Dead concert, because a Dead concert is positive anarchy, onstage and off. Although the Grateful Dead emerged out of, and are still largely identified with, the countercultural fringes of the psychedelic 1960s, their musical roots go straight to the heart of America, mixing rhythm and blues classics with folksy ballads and their own inimitable brands of surging percussion and intrepid space. In any mode, the band's improvisational approach concentrates on the making of music, not merely performing songs, and the audience's unbridled enthusiasm urges them on to ever higher highs.

The Grateful Dead have made a career out of playing popular music, but have done so almost entirely on their own terms. In a music industry that's based on selling records, in which live performance is carefully choreographed to showcase a band's latest release, Grateful Dead are as unlikely a bunch of pop stars you could think of. In conventional pop music terms, they've gone about it all wrong, focusing in on each performance as it happens, without much concern for presenting a saleable 'image', much less for the vagaries of musical 'style'. They play the music as they feel it, and never play the same song the same way twice. Some of the more evangelical fans of the Grateful Dead have fought for years against mainstream misunderstanding, but although the band's current mass success has encouraged many a 'told you so' attitude – 'If you think *this* is hot, you shoulda seen 'em at the Fillmore in April '71' – for every proselytizing Deadhead a dozen more would be happy to keep the band all to themselves. 'Misfit Power' is guitarist Bob Weir's name for the band's phenomenal magnetism. However you explain it, they must be on to something, because for the past decade Grateful Dead have been the most successful live band in the world, playing to over a million fans a year with hardly a ticket left unsold. After 25 years on the rock 'n' roll rollercoaster, Grateful Dead are still alive and kicking, and making music as only they can.

Gene Anthony

HISTORY OF THE GRATEFUL DEAD

The early years of the ongoing chaos that is the Grateful Dead were full of starts, stops, and sidetracks running off in innumerable parallel and sometimes contradictory directions. To unravel all the various strands would take teams of detectives with the combined talents of Sherlock Holmes and Grigori Rasputin, but even a brief dig is worthwhile since so many of the things that happened then have had an enormous impact upon the evolving shapes and sounds of the band.

It's hard to say what it was about the suburbs of 1950s San Francisco that shaped the young minds of the nascent Grateful Dead, but the musicians who came together to play in the band all spent their formative years within shouting distance of the Golden Gate Bridge. At a time when most of America was enjoying the fruits of post-war prosperity, liking Ike and looking forward to squeeky clean futures, San Francisco, during the 1950s, was alive with the manic energy of the Beat Generation. While writers like Jack Kerouac, William Burroughs and Allen Ginsberg were opening up whole new literary horizons, musicians filled smokey underground clubs with the cool sounds of Be-bop and Breakout jazz in impromptu all-night jam sessions. Although much of the drunken hellraising had died down by the time Grateful Dead were old enough to join in, by the early 1960s the spirit had evolved into a thriving folk music scene around the Bay Area's two main college campuses, the University of California at Berkeley and Stanford University near Palo Alto, twenty miles south of San Francisco proper. It was in and among the late-night coffee houses of Palo Alto, where young turks read 'On The Road', played guitars and listened to Bob Dylan records, that the Grateful Dead first came into being.

Many of the band members knew each other for years before they all got together, but the longest-enduring of the Grateful Dead musical relationships is that of the main songwriting duo, Jerry Garcia and the reclusive lyricist Robert Hunter. The two met in

Gene Anthony

Gene Anthony

1961, fresh out of short stints in the U.S. Army, and by the next year they were playing together regularly in a variety of folksy bluegrass bands with names like the Thunder Mountain Tub Thumpers and the Black Mountain Boys. As the local music scene was small and closely knit, it didn't take long for Garcia and Co. to come to the attention of R 'n' B fanatic Ron 'Pigpen' McKernan, whose father, Phil, was famous in the area for his late-night radio program. Pigpen – a name bestowed upon him by Garcia – took to hanging out at the old chateau that Garcia shared with a half-dozen other South Bay musicians, and joined in on the nightly jam sessions. Garcia was so impressed with the wild-looking 16-year-old's passionate harmonica playing (and by his gravelly, intensely emotional vocals) that Pigpen and he joined, as lead singer and frontman respectively, Troy Weidenheimer's energetic electric blues band called the Zodiacs.

To complete the lineup the Zodiacs needed a drummer, and Garcia knew who to ask. Playing in small clubs on weekends didn't pay very much, so to make ends meet Garcia had found work teaching banjo and guitar in a Palo Alto music shop, Dana Morgan Music. The drum teacher there was one Bill Kreutzmann who, though still in high school, was already playing in a handful of local rock bands, and soon enough was pounding away behind Garcia and Pigpen.

The same music shop also provided the setting for Bob Weir's entry into this charmed circle. Weir had been playing guitar in a number of high school rock groups – one, called the Uncalled Four, had played a gig with one of Garcia and Hunter's bands – but was still restless and bored. As he tells it, 'On New Year's Eve 1963, a friend of mine and I were wandering the backstreets of Palo Alto . . . we were way too young to get into any of the hot clubs. We walked by the back door of this music store we used to frequent . . . and we heard banjo music. This seemed strange to us 'cause it was New Year's Eve, so we knocked on the door . . . it was Garcia, who was the local hot banjo player. We knew he had the key to the front of the shop, so we talked him into breaking in, and we grabbed a couple of the guitars we'd always wanted to play.'

After playing till the early hours they decided to throw together a jug band, then a popular format in which guitars and banjos were backed up by a bizarre assortment of jugs, bottles, washtubs and other homemade percussion instruments. Jerry and Bobby, joined by Pigpen and a half dozen others, played around Palo Alto a number of times, as Mother McGee's Uptown Jug Champions, throughout 1964. As Garcia remembers, 'Our jug band was complete and total anarchy. Just lots and lots of people in it, and Pigpen and Bob and I were more or less the ringleaders. We'd work out various kinds of musically funny material. It was like a musical vacation to get on stage and have a good time.'

Just when interest in the jug band began to wane, along came the British Invasion: the Beatles, the Yardbirds, and especially the raunchy R 'n' B of the Rolling Stones. 'We could do that,' said Pigpen, and so the band went electric, again enlisting Bill on drums and now calling themselves the Warlocks. The problem of finding equipment was solved when Dana Morgan Jr., son of the owner of the music store, joined the band as bass player, and his dad donated all the necessary and costly gear. Dana didn't last long, though, and in a flash of inspiration Garcia asked his friend Phil Lesh to take his place.

Phil, the only academically trained musician of the bunch – and the one with perfect pitch – had studied music theory and composition at UC Berkeley and with Luciano Berio at Mills College in Oakland (minimalist composer Steve Reich was also in the class, and is still a friend), but had never touched an electric guitar before he played in the band. He'd got to know Garcia when both were hanging around wealthy Stanford students, preying on their young minds and raiding their refrigerators. The friendship was cemented when Phil, who at the time was working as an engineer at KPFA radio station, recorded a session of Garcia's banjo playing for a folk music program.

With Phil on bass and Bill on drums backing up Pig on keyboards, Bobby on rhythm and Jerry on lead guitar, the Warlocks settled into a stable format and began gigging regularly in bars and pizza parlours around the Bay Area. The Warlocks, however, were anything but your normal bar band; not only did they play louder and longer than anyone else, things also started getting weird. 'The bartenders were crazy. We'd be playing and they'd line the bars with ashtrays, fill them with lighter fluid and light them,' Weir recalled. 'The whole bar would seemingly go up in flames and the place would get pretty crazy for a minute, so we'd pick louder and more intense.'

While the Warlocks were getting up to strange things along the bay, another group was doing similarly bizarre things in the redwood groves of the hills above, at the La Honda house of writer Ken Kesey, whose first book, 'One Flew over the Cuckoo's Nest', was a brilliant critical and commercial success. This band of oddballs took to calling themselves the Merry Pranksters, and travelled around the Bay Area and across the country in the self-contained comfort of a day-glo painted school bus, dressing up in outrageous costumes and acting out cinematic fantasies on the streets of America.

One of Kesey's best friends, and the driver of the legendary bus, was the one and only Neal Cassady, the man upon whom Jack Kerouac had modelled Dean Moriarty, hero of his Beat epic 'On the Road'. Despite the larger than life mythology Kerouac built up around him, Cassady was, if anything, a more astonishing man in the flesh. First as a literary character of almost unbelievable drive and power, and later as an equally dynamic figure on the San Francisco underground scene, hé was a major inspiration to many of the Warlocks. Garcia in particular was impressed: 'The resonance of meeting this guy who was, as a fictional figure, a model for a lot of people, was intense. Neal was totally original, and way more that person than you could've imagined. There

Ken Kesey at an Acid Test

Gene Anthony

was nobody like him; he expanded the possibilities, changed the fabric of the world.'

That the Warlocks and the Merry Pranksters – two bands of outward bound, mind-altered misfits – would get together was probably inevitable considering the overlap of interests, and the very few people (in 1965, at least) doing anything at all out of the ordinary. Once the contact was made however, it was made for good, and the Warlocks soon became fixtures at the madcap parties taking place at the Kesey spread. The main thing that brought the two tribes together was their mutual interest in exploring and enjoying the weird and wonderful world of the newly available, little known and still legal hallucinogenic drug, LSD. Ironically, 'Acid' had first been introduced locally by none other than the U.S. government in the early 1960s, when C.I.A. sponsored scientists at Stanford recruited volunteers for a series of tests aimed at quantifying the effect various substances – mescaline, psylocybe mushrooms, LSD – would have on the behavior of a handful of otherwise normal, bright young things. Both Kesey and Robert Hunter had taken part in the trials, and afterward they and their cronies continued to do so some extracurricular research in the comfort of their own homes.

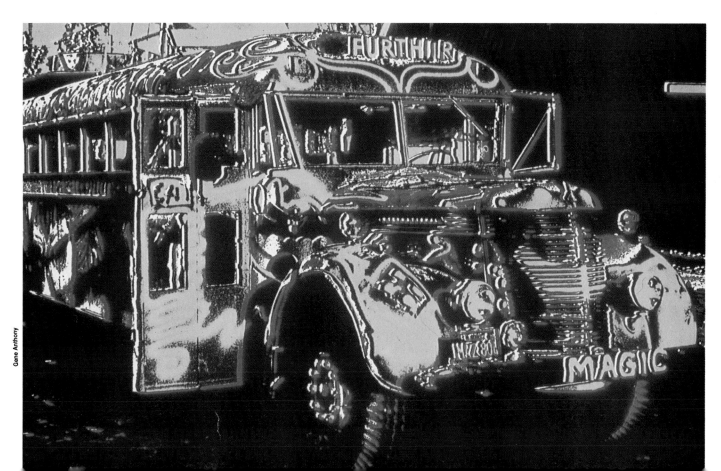

Gene Anthony

Acid Tests, 1966

The Acid Tests

Convinced by a powerful if still undefined feeling that they were indeed on to something, the Pranksters and the Grateful Dead took their private parties to the people, setting out to find other like-minded souls through the 'multi-media orgies' they christened the Acid Tests. The Acid Tests, advertised with intriguing come-ons like 'Can you pass the Acid Test?' on posters placed in bookshops and cafes, were at once carefully prepared but also entirely spontaneous undertakings in which guitars, drums, light shows, chain saws, performances, props, costumes, keyboards – and most of all, a freely-available supply of LSD – were all just tools, useful for shaping and directing an evening's flights of fancy. There was no overall plan; anything could happen, once you'd arrived at the site. The one guiding principle was that anything goes, the only requirement that each person present was somehow to push things to the edge and see what would happen. No one was to be a spectator – everyone took part, however they saw fit. Throughout each Test, the Grateful Dead were there, sometimes playing, other times not, enjoying the space the setup gave them but always pushing to see what could be done with it.

The actual Acid Tests were held between December 1965 and March 1966. After a few private practice sessions at La Honda, and another in Santa Cruz, the first public Test was held at a ramshackle old house on the outskirts of San Jose, where the evening's festivities regularly ground to a halt as the ageing electrical system blew fuse after fuse. Over the next two months a dozen further events took place all over the West Coast, from Watts to Portland, each heading off in its own direction and none ever ending until dawn the next day.

It's not surprising that no one has ever really 'captured' what it was about the Tests that so affected the people who were involved in them. Tom Wolfe probably came the closest with his book, 'The Electric Kool-Aid Acid Test':

The very ooze of cellular Creation seems to ectoplast into the ethers and then the Dead coming in with their immense submarine vibrato vibrating, garanging, from the Aleutian rocks to the baja griffing cliffs of the Gulf of California. The Dead's weird sound! agony-in-ecstasis! submarine somehow, turbid half the time, tremendously loud but like sitting under a waterfall, at the same time full of sort of ghoul-show vibrato sounds as if each string on their electric guitars is half a block long and twanging in a room full of natural gas, not to mention their great Hammond electric organ, which sounds like a movie house Wurlitzer, a diathermy machine, a Citizen's Band radio and an Auto-Grind garbage truck at 4 am, all coming in over the same frequency . . .

No doubt, you probably had to have been there to get it, but it would be wrong to think it was just the drugs which made it all come alive. A whole lot of big ideas, ideas about music and art and the meaning of life, were floating around then, ideas that in many ways shaped what the Grateful Dead strive to be and to do. It's hardly stretching the point to say that whatever attitude, or philosophical stance, Grateful Dead take toward their musical activities, the roots of their collective creativity were firmly set in the fertile soil of these Tests, and it's likewise safe to say that the events had a fundamental impact upon the band, as individuals and as a musical entity.

As Garcia later explained: 'The Acid Test was the prototype of our whole basic trip, but nothing has ever come up to the level of the way the Acid Test was. It's just never been equalled . . . It was something more incredible than just rock and roll and a light show; it was just a million times more incredible. It was incredible because of the formlessness, because of the thing of people wandering around wondering what was going on . . . and stuff happening spontaneously and people being prepared to accept any kind of thing that was happening, and to add to it. Everybody was creating. Everybody was doing everything. That's about the simplest explanation.'

Acid Tests, 1966

Gene Anthony

The Name of the Band is . . . Grateful Dead

Charged by the creative energies that were unleashed in the interchange between the Pranksters and the Warlocks – and also because Phil had come across another band using the same name – the Warlocks were moved to find a new moniker for themselves. Various alternatives were mooted but none seemed quite to fit the spirit of the adventure until, while lounging around one afternoon at Phil's house, Garcia hit upon this entry while leafing through the dictionary. Under 'Grateful Dead', it read

> *The motif of folk tales which begin with the hero coming upon a group of people ill-treating or refusing to bury the corpse of a man who had died without paying his debts. He gives his last penny, either to pay the man's debts or to give him a decent funeral. Within a few hours he meets with a travelling companion who aids him in some impossible task, wins him a fortune or saves his life. The story ends with the companion disclosing himself as the man whose corpse the hero had befriended.*

Taking the phrase in the sense of cyclical change rather than some sort of morbidity, it proved just the thing for our heroes. After the first few events the freewheeling Acid Tests inevitably lost some of their 'formlessness' and with it began to lose their edge. As the crowds got larger – and more intent on being entertained – the shows became more and more formalized, and gradually came to resemble what now seems like a typical rock concert, with the Grateful Dead as the main attraction. The surge of popularity was shown by the success of the Trips Festivals, the first of which was held in January 1966. A key moment in the growth of the San Francisco music scene, the shows garnered media attention and, equally important, proved that there was money to be made out of what was becoming known as the Psychedelic Scene. Soon new venues like the Fillmore Auditorium and Avalon Ballroom were holding concerts every weekend to cater to the growing crowds of fans,

Herb Greene

and hundreds of kids were heading to the Haight-Ashbury district of San Francisco, the plexus of this emerging sub-culture. By September 1966 many of the Dead were living more or less full time at 710 Ashbury, a large rooming house looked after by their then-manager Danny Rifkin, just off the famous intersection that gave its name to the Haight-Ashbury neighborhood. Pigpen was the first to move in, and though it wasn't planned this way, the other residents moved out soon after, making space for the band and associates. The house became a headquarters and meeting place, and as often as not was alive to the sounds of yet another impromptu session. As the number of listeners grew in the course of an afternoon, these shows would often drift down to the nearby Panhandle, a narrow section of Golden Gate Park so called because it jutted out from the park into the surrounding city. On Sundays, or whenever the mood struck them, the band would hire a generator and a flatbed truck and play for free to crowds of two hundred or so in Speedway Meadows, in the heart of the spacious park.

Gene Anthony

1967 started off with a bang, and continued to explode throughout the year, growing by leaps and bounds until the whole world seemed to have their eyes and ears trained on San Francisco's happening new heart – the Haight Ashbury. Bill Graham's Fillmore Auditorium and the Family Dog's Avalon Ballroom were holding rock shows six days a week, advertised all over town by strikingly beautiful posters, and every other shop on Haight Street seemed to be selling hippie garb. Tour bus companies even began running sightseeing trips – called the Hippie Hop – around the Haight for tourists to gawk at the wayward youth, for despite the fact that LSD had been declared illegal by the California legislature in October 1966, the psychedelic scene continued to thrive. Young people headed for San Francisco from all over the world to take part in the Summer of Love. Many of them found part-time jobs – the Post Office was one of the main sources of funds – and places to stay in the rambling old Victorian houses that the 'hippies' turned into experiments in communal living.

However well these alternative arrangements worked out on a personal level, signs of trouble were becoming increasingly apparent, not least because many of the newcomers were under-age, underfunded, and generally unprepared for life on their own. All in all over 100,000 kids arrived in the first six months of 1967, more than doubling the population of the Haight-Ashbury district and placing an increasing strain on the already stretched resources of what was in many ways just another urban neighborhood.

That things stayed in good spirits as long as they did was largely down to the efforts of the Diggers, an altruistic and absurdist street theater group who took their name from a 17th Century anarchist farming community in England. Besides staging guerrilla theater pieces on the streets of San Francisco, the Diggers also ran the Free Store – at which they offered up old clothes and furniture scrounged from rubbish tips – and organised free meals for hundreds of people at 4pm every afternoon in the

Panhandle of Golden Gate Park. Grateful Dead opened 1967 with a New Year's Day benefit to raise money for their efforts.

The first undeniable proof that something out of the ordinary was emerging in the Haight was the Human Be-in – also known as A Gathering of the Tribes, and advertised as 'the joyful, face-to-face beginning of the new epoch' – on January 14, which attracted some 20,000 people to Golden Gate Park. A remarkable event in many ways, it showed the authorities that thousands of hippies and like-minded souls could get together for a peaceful day of partying, drinking and dancing. As Jay Stevens describes the scene in his book 'Storming Heaven',

> *mostly there were hippies, looking as though they had ransacked the prop room of a particularly cheesy summer theater, wandering around in serapes and desert robes and Victorian petticoats and paisley bodystockings, bedecked with bells and flowers, young boys with nastursiums wagging from their ears and at least one gray-haired grandmother with a rose tied to her cane. They sat and listened to the poetry, they danced to the Grateful Dead, they craned their necks to get a better look at Timothy Leary, they jeered when someone cut the trunk cord from the main generator, silencing the stage, and they cheered when the power was restored.*

Everyone had a good time, even the Hell's Angels, who were there as stewards but

> *spent most of their time entertaining children who had wandered away from their parents . . . What a sight : the hardest outlaw bikers in the free world clowning around on the ground like a bunch of old daycare pros.*

In March the band's debut LP *The Grateful Dead* was released on Warner Brothers Records, having been recorded in a manic three-day session in Los Angeles early in the year. On it the band raced through versions of the bluesy staples they'd been playing for the past year, like *Good Mornin Little Schoolgirl* and *Beat in on Down the Line*, which has always been a live favorite. They also included two original tunes: Garcia's *Cream Puff War* and the

Human Be-in, Jan 14, 1967

lively band composition *The Golden Road*, Grateful Dead's first single, the lyrics of which give a good sense of what the band was all about:

> *Everybody's dancing in a ring around the sun*
> *Nobody's finished, we ain't even begun*
> *So take off your shoes child, and take off your hat*
> *Try on your wings, and find out where it's at.*
> *°Hey hey, come right away, join the party, party everyday . . .*

That summer the Dead took their show on the road, playing free afternoon concerts in New York City's Tompkins Square and Central Park during a week of shows at the sweaty Cafe a Go-Go club. They returned home in time to play at the Monterey International Pop Festival on June 18, a landmark event in many histories of West Coast music. Lots of famous names, including

Jimi Hendrix, Otis Redding and the Who, were on the bill and a film was made by D. A. Pennebaker, but the Dead were put off by the slickness of the L.A. music moguls who promoted the event. The band had expected that some of the substantial amount of money made would go to various worthy causes but when the organisers, led by John Phillips of the Mamas and the Papas, said no, the Grateful Dead refused to be in the concert film or on the album. When the organisers further refused to make tickets available to the thousands who'd come down from San Francisco, Grateful Dead borrowed the concert PA system the night before the festival and played a free show with Steve Miller's Blues Band at a nearby college.

The band returned to the Haight to play the first of their more or less annual Summer Solstice concerts, but it was much changed from the way it had been. By the time 'Time' discovered the Haight and presented it to the nation on their July 7 cover, the thousands of young people who'd heard about it through the grapevine had already proved easy game for ripoff artists and drug dealers. The national exposure served only to worsen what was already a dire situation and in order to reassert their control, the San Francisco civic authorities banned live performances in the Golden Gate Park.

Early in October the heat came close to home as SFPD drugs squad officers raided the band's premises at 710 Ashbury, backed by a full contingent of local TV and newspaper reporters. After forcing their way inside they arrested Bob Weir and Pigpen as well as band equipment chief Bob Matthews, manager Rock Scully and a half dozen other friends. The band's stature was such that the arrest was front page news on the main San Francisco 'Chronicle' paper. Since charges were soon dropped, however, the event would probably have been quickly forgotten were it not for the extensive coverage given to it in the inaugural November 9, 1967 edition of pop music magazine 'Rolling Stone'. The Stone version of events presented the arrestees as victims of police harrassment, quoting extensively from Rifkin's statement to the press: 'The people who enforce the law use it almost exclusively against individuals who threaten their ideas of the way people should look and act. The Grateful Dead are people engaged in constructive, creative effort in the musical field, and this house is where we work as well as our residence. Because the police fear and misinterpret us, our effort is now interrupted as we deal with the consequences of a harrassing arrest.'

Whatever the media reaction the band treated the arrests as probably inevitable, but more or less laughable. Their attention was much more focused upon their second album, which was to be the Grateful Dead's first serious foray into writing their own

Busted...but unbowed. Press Conference at 710

Danny Rifkin speaks up for the band

songs and a radical departure from conventional record industry practice. Some of these songs had already been introduced into the live act, but the biggest change around this time was the addition of percussionist Mickey Hart to the lineup – in the middle of a show on September 29.

1968 was a year of violent upheaval, in absolute contrast to the Haight-Ashbury dreams of peace and love of a year before. First Martin Luther King then Bobby Kennedy were assassinated, the streets of America erupted in riots, and the very fabric of American society seemed on the verge of being torn asunder by an undeclared war in Southeast Asia. For the Grateful Dead, who'd moved out of the Haight into the more open spaces of rural Marin County, north of San Francisco, the year brought far more positive changes. The band opened their own performing space, the Carousel Ballroom, and broadened their musical horizons by starting to write their own material, stepping away from their blues renditions into a much more wild and original musical world – Grateful Dead classics like *The Other One*, *St. Stephen* and especially *Dark Star* all stem from this period.

Two forces began to influence the Grateful Dead's music in 1968. New initiate Mickey Hart's powerful drumming enabled the dynamic percussion duo to experiment with unusual rhythms and patterns that no single player could handle on his own. As Kreutzmann said, 'We're not trying to be two drummers, we're trying to be one drummer with eight arms'. From the start the two drummers had an uncanny knack of knowing exactly what the other was about to do, and quickly began to experiment with

odd time signatures, some of which were so distinctive they gave their name to new songs – *The Eleven, The Seven, The Main Ten*. The other noticeable change was the emergence of Robert Hunter as the band's wordsmith and lyricist. Hunter had been a friend of the Dead from the very beginning but had drifted away, returning fortuitously just as the band were beginning to write their own songs. One of the first and most distinctive pieces to come out of this turbocharged musical alliance was nothing less than *Dark Star*. This all-time great Dead opus became the core of the band's performances as it developed and expanded, its structural simplicity allowing the tune to absorb countless improvised permutations.

As the band became more confident about their musicianship, they also became more bold and independent in their approach to recording. After their dissatisfying debut (the band have never thought much of any of their recorded work), the Grateful Dead set about trying to introduce some of the excitement and fluidity of their live act onto vinyl. This they did by taping a number of their shows, which they then mixed together, often one on top of another, adding layer upon layer to form a side-long waterfall of sound and fury. *That's it for the Other One* was the overall title they gave to this ambitious multi-part composition, which fills the opening side of *Anthem of the Sun*, their second album, released in July 1968. An exception to the overall lyrical abstruseness of the LP is the Weir and Kreutzman penned second section, which serves as Grateful Dead's memorial to their old friend and Acid Test comrade Neal Cassady, who was found dead in Mexico early in the year. The second side has Pigpen singing lead on two comparatively straightforward R 'n' B tunes, *Alligator* followed by *Caution: Do Not Stop on Tracks*, both of which intercut between assorted live versions joined by extended jams and highlighted by Garcia's overdubbed and ultra-sharp lead guitar. 1969 was the busiest year yet for the Grateful Dead clan. Not only did they come out with two of their most distinctive albums, they also played more shows, including the epic Woodstock

festival, than ever before.

Grateful Dead's third album, *Aoxomoxoa*, which came out in June, took to new frontiers the experimental techniques the band had begun toying with on *Anthem*. Fascination with studio gadgets and techniques – it was among the first 16-track records ever made – coupled with their perfectionist approach turned it into their most bizarre, and costly, recording ever. Much of it sounds like it's from another planet, and few of the songs lasted very long in the live show. Even *St. Stephen*, which opens the LP and has the most comprehensible lyrics, 'has some real goofy shit in it', as Garcia told 'Golden Road' magazine. Many of the others – like the spacey *Mountains of the Moon*, featuring Phil's music school friend Tom Constanten on harpsichord – seem weird just for the sake of being weird, and the album's complexities take some getting used to. Phil dominates much of the playing, his bass lines snaking through the arresting rhythm of *China Cat Sunflower*, the one song that's survived in the live repertoire.

'The only message in our music is - Think For Yourself'

Robert Hunter

Mary Ann Mayer

Though *Anthem of the Sun* was a respectable seller it came nowhere near earning back its advance, and by the time the Grateful Dead were finished with *Aoxomoxoa* the band owed Warner Brothers some $200,000. Fortunately they had another record ready for release, one that was so far from their studio work it's hard to believe they were recorded at more or less the same time. *Live Dead*, a two record set, proved that whatever complexities the band got up to in the studio, they were still able to crank it up and kick ass on stage. The songs on the album, recorded at the Fillmore West in February 1969, are presented on disc as they were in concert, without overdubs and almost unedited. The real gem of the disc is the Dead's workout on *Dark Star*, twenty minutes of Grateful Dead at their improvisational best. The record also showcases Pigpen doing his thing to *Lovelight*, the R 'n' B classic that was the irresistible crowdpleaser of late '60s Grateful Dead shows.

Jim Marshall

In between putting out the records Grateful Dead found time to play over 130 shows, culminating in an appearance at the Woodstock festival. For anyone who was there, and for millions more who weren't, Woodstock was the event of an eventful decade, if not a lifetime. But the Dead gave possibly the worst performance of their career. A torrential downpour shorted out the sound system and, after a few hours' delay for repairs, the Dead started to play. As Garcia remembers it, 'people were leaning across my amps and saying stuff like "the stage is collapsing", it was just awful. That part I'd just as soon forget... but the rest of it was great fun. We had a swell time above and beyond that. The *eventness* of it was very apparent even there, as though history was looking at it. I felt like it was crowded with invisible time travellers from the future.'

No account of 1960s San Francisco can end without a mention of that decade's most notorious event, the ill-fated Rolling Stones concert at Altamont Speedway forty miles east of San Francisco on December 6 1969. Famous because of the 'Gimme Shelter' concert film shot there, and infamous because a fan was stabbed to death in front of the stage, everything about the show, from the lack of preparation to the utter absence of even the most basic facilities at the site, boded ill; in retrospect the show should never have gone on. But because of their standing in the San Francisco music scene (the Dead had lent some of their equipment, and were going to play but didn't) Grateful Dead were blamed for the fiasco, as if somehow they should have done something to stop it from going wrong. After the high of Woodstock, no one foresaw the downer Altamont turned into.

Grateful Dead charged into the 1970s in overdrive, playing more shows in more places than in any year before or since. 'We were working our asses off,' says Garcia, explaining how the band managed to do 145 shows in 23 states – plus their first gig in Europe – and still have enough left in them to conquer the FM airwaves with a pair of albums, *Workingman's Dead* and *American Beauty*, marking yet another new direction for the band.

Jim Marshall

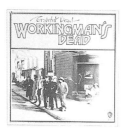

Amid all the demands of being on the road for weeks at a time, it's hard to know where Grateful Dead found time to write and record but it proved to be one of their most creative periods. After the studio space of *Aoxomoxoa*, and the extended improvisations on *Live Dead*, Garcia suggested making a good, cheap album. 'Why don't we approach our next record like a Country and Western record, go after absolute simplicity in the recording, and do simple songs that aren't going to take us forever to learn and to work out?' Fortunately, Grateful Dead were already working on just the right songs for this no-frills treatment, having come under the harmonizing influence of Crosby, Stills and Nash, who were frequent guests at Mickey Hart's Marin County ranch. It's Garcia you hear playing pedal steel guitar on the CSN hit *Teach Your Children*, and it was through them that the Grateful Dead began to gain confidence in the musical power of their own voices.

The first outward sign of a return to their roots was the band's beginning to do an acoustic set in the middle of a show, sandwiched between a fairly straight opening and a sometimes very spacey final set. The acoustic set gave the band a chance to work on the songs – *Uncle John's Band, Dire Wolf, Casey Jones, Friend of the Devil* – which were much more like what they'd been doing in their earlier, folksy incarnations in the coffee houses of Palo Alto.

The end result of all this was a real breakthrough for the band: *Workingman's Dead*, about which everything, from the grainy cover shot to the pared-down arrangements to the work-a-day concerns expressed in the lyrics, marks a definite move back to basics. None more so than *Cumberland Blues*, the rollicking bluegrass tune about hardworking Appalachian miners that's most likely a metaphor for the itinerant musician's life, especially in its rhyming refrain:

> **Gotta get down to the Cumberland Mine**
> **That's where I mainly spend my time**
> **Make good money, five dollars a day**
> **Make any more I might move away**

For the first time in their musical lives, Grateful Dead were going in the same direction, if still not at the forefront, of mainstream pop music. Even the Rolling Stones were doing country rock tunes! As Robert Hunter later commented, '*Workingman's Dead* took us from nowheresville to at least semi-somewheresville as far as the public was concerned.' The songs got more airplay, mainly on the emerging 'album rock' FM radio stations, than any previous Grateful Dead releases, and the record has ever since been one of their all-time bestsellers.

The band's inroads into popular success were made secure by their next release, *American Beauty*, the cover of which can also be read as *American Reality*. Of a piece with *Workingman's Dead*, and again featuring delicate, multipart harmonies, the tunes on this November 1970 release are some of the catchiest and most

melodic Grateful Dead have ever come up with. From the opening track *Box of Rain*, the rarely performed Phil Lesh tune that's many a Deadhead's favorite song, all the way through to the largely autobiographical, 'life on the road' anthem of the single *Truckin* – which shot straight to Number One, in Turlock, California – the album is packed full of classic Grateful Dead tracks: *Friend of the Devil*, *Ripple*, and *Brokedown Palace*, to name just three more.

After the generally upbeat previous year, 1971 was a bit of a downer for the Grateful Dead, beginning with Mickey Hart's departure for personal reasons. Another worrying aspect of the year was the sudden closing in the middle of the year of both the Fillmores, East and West, which had been their second homes.

But before the Fillmore East closed, and just after Mickey left, in February 1971 the band recorded what was to become the Dead's first gold record, a live, two record set that Phil wanted to call *Skullfuck*, but which Warner Brothers put out as simply *Grateful Dead*. It was also known, for its cover art, as *Skull 'n' Roses*.

Irrespective of the wrangling that went on over its name it is at times a dynamically energetic session, one that featured sharp versions of Grateful Dead standards such as *Going Down the Road Feeling Bad* out of *Not Fade Away* and introduced a number of new songs into the repertoire, including especially killer versions of both the haunting ballad *Wharf Rat* and the riproaring *Bertha*. It's also one of the few albums the band has admitted to liking. As Garcia said after its release: 'It's *us*, man. It's the prototype Grateful Dead, basic unit. Each one of those tracks is the total picture … enough of an overview so people can see we're a regular shoot-em-up saloon band.'

Though Kreutzmann was able to cover for the missing Hart, the band was put under an increasing personal and musical burden as Pigpen's health deteriorated, forcing him to miss a number of shows as the year went on. This shrunk the band down to a quartet for various shows, which meant that each player had to carry a lot more of each song, and so was less able to cut loose and play freely, which has always been a hallmark of the Grateful Dead. To remedy the situation, in September they signed up Keith Godchaux, a Bay Area native who'd been playing piano in a few bands, to play keyboards. His singer wife Donna joined at the end of the year.

The *Skull 'n' Roses* live album came out in October, and to support its release Warners arranged to have that fall's shows broadcast live over local FM radio stations. It was a simply brilliant ploy, one which got their music into places it otherwise might never have reached, and cemented the band's reputation as a dynamic and powerful live attraction. Sadly, just as the tour kicked off, the band suffered the loss of another friend and musical partner when Duane Allman died, only a year after the death of their longtime buddy Janis Joplin.

On a brighter note Pigpen returned to the lineup in December, singing and playing harmonica.

'He was so inventive - he played some jazz stuff and free music that was just incredible. He had a heart of music.'

Bill Kreutzmann on Keith Godchaux

Mary Ann Mayer

1972 was dominated by the band's tour of Europe, a crazy affair that found the band and forty-plus fellow travelers larking across the continent in finest Prankster fashion. The sixteen performances in six different countries were all recorded for posterity, and, whatever the reason, the band was in tiptop form. In fact, they were so good that, after listening to the tapes, the band decided to release a three-record set complete with full colour booklet of tour photos, to let the folks back home see what Grateful Dead had got up to. The album, titled simply *Europe '72*, was their best yet. As Garcia says, 'We really played well in Europe, and the tone, the sound of the band was terrific there. We played some wonderful rooms, some of the finest concert halls in Europe, so the ambient sound is really lovely, really nice.'

The album showcased some of the best vocals the band has ever managed – even if some *were* overdubbed. Their harmonies have never been sweeter than on tunes like *I Know You Rider* (which melts magically out of a brilliant *China Cat Sunflower*) and *Sugar Magnolia*. *Europe '72* also introduced a couple of crankably hot new tunes that have been Deadhead favorites ever since: *Brown-Eyed Women*, *Ramble on Rose*, and Weir's earth-rattling rocker *One More Saturday Night*.

Before they set off for the Olde Worlde on April Fool's Day, Grateful Dead members had already released one solo album and recorded another both of which, though entirely different from one another, contain many tunes that fit in straightaway to the Grateful Dead set. In January Garcia released *Garcia* (also known as *The Wheel*), a solo album in almost every sense of the word. Jerry played every instrument but drums (provided by Kreutzmann), proving once again his mastery over anything with strings on it. The songs, all of which were written with Hunter, are all excellent, from *Deal* to *Bird Song* to *Sugaree* to *Loser* – and that's just the first side! In contrast to Garcia's solo effort, Bob Weir's first solo album, *Ace*, was solo in name only, as almost every track was backed by a more or less complete contingent of

Rosie McGee Ende

none other than the Grateful Dead. Like *Garcia* the album contains a number of great tracks, as well as marking the beginning of Bobby's collaboration with his lyricist and old school friend John Barlow. The standouts, besides the cantina rocker *Mexicali Blues*, are the two closing songs; first the riproaring *Playing in the Band* then the poignant *Cassidy*, a song written and named for the newborn daughter of Eileen Law, who ran (and runs) the Dead Head fan liaison organisation.

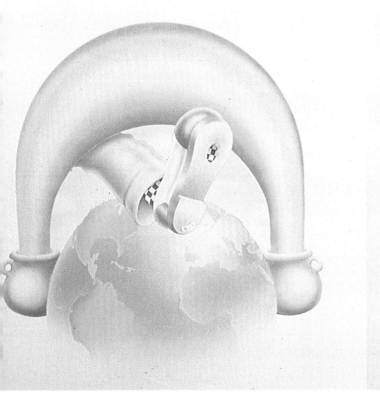 

1973 was a year of major changes for Grateful Dead, as it was the year the band finally made the long-hoped-for break from the multinational music business and set up entirely on their own. After a year or more of tinkering and talking about it, the Grateful Dead set up an organisation that could handle every aspect of Grateful Dead in-house. From recording in their own studio – Le Club Front – to marketing and distributing their records (through Grateful Dead Records) to making travel and tour arrangements (through Fly-by-Night Travel) everything was done by an ever-growing Grateful Dead operation.

Sadly, while the expanding Grateful Dead organisation signalled the band's optimism for the future, one important figure would not be there to share it. On March 8 1973, Ron 'Pigpen' McKernan died at his Marin County home, aged 27. Those close to him had hoped he would return to good health, since he had been obeying doctors' orders and staying off the booze, but it was too little too late to make up for the years of abuse to which he had subjected his body. He went out in fitting style, though, decked out in motorcycle leathers and wearing the colors of the San Francisco Hell's Angels, who also provided a guard of honor as the cortege made its way to the cemetery. The wake which followed was a raucous but respectful affair, which the Dead broke off an East Coast tour to attend.

The band's last album before leaving Warner Bros was a fitting tribute to their fallen companion. *Bear's Choice – A History of the Grateful Dead Vol 1* captures Pigpen at his best, growling out R 'n' B classics like *Hard to Handle* and *Smokestack Lightning*. The record also includes some oddities, considering how much archival material was available, like a rare and unlikely *Wake Up Little Susie*, a song the Grateful Dead only ever played a dozen times.

The big test of the viability of the Dead's mad dash toward independence was the release of *Wake of the Flood*, their first album on their own Grateful Dead Records, and their first studio album since *American Beauty* three years before. The LP was made incredibly quickly – just two months from beginning recording to the release – and every aspect of its production, manufacture and distribution was handled under the eagle eyes of quality-conscious Grateful Dead personnel.

Many of the songs on the album, which was snapped up by eager Deadheads, are variations on the theme of breaking away and starting afresh. There are also numerous references to crossing rivers, and of course to floods, both Biblical and real. Side one builds slowly through the jangling *Mississippi Half-step Uptown Tudeloo* and *Let Me Sing Your Blues Away* – Keith Godchaux's only

lead vocal – into the mournful *Row Jimmy*, struggling against a rising tide of lameness. The lovely *Stella Blue*, a song that 'just popped out full grown', closes the side, but the poignant tone is quickly wiped out by the second side's upbeat *Here Comes Sunshine*, which blazes the way for the uplifting *Eyes of the World*, with its sparkling guitars and optimistic lyrics. Bob Weir is in fine voice on his impressive contribution, the side-ending *Weather Report Suite*, with some energetic horn work by Martin Fierro.

Early in 1974 the Grateful Dead started work on the follow-up LP, which came out in the middle of the year. The album *Grateful Dead From the Mars Hotel*, which took its title from a derelict hotel in San Francisco, is much more song-oriented than its predecessor. Jump-starting with *U.S. Blues* – whose irresistible beat has made it a natural encore tune – it quickly changes tack into the fragile *China Doll*, then into Phil's last lead vocal, the evocative *Unbroken Chain*. The undisputed highlight is the side two opener, the only recorded version of the lovely *Scarlet Begonias*. But the album also includes one of the most un-Deadlike songs imaginable, the jaded, somewhat misogynist *Money Money* – though exactly why this song is so objectionable and why *Dupree's Diamond Blues* is so well-loved is hard to say.

That Grateful Dead included it might, however, give some insight into the stress and strain the band was under, given the incessant pressure of their ever-expanding organisation. Nick-named Urobourus after the mythical beast which grew larger and larger by devouring itself, the band's tendency to lend support to all sorts of new endeavors – hiring blimps so they could play in inaccessible outdoor locations, researching a prototype CD technology that took the form of holographic pyramids and more seriously the massive 'Wall of Sound' PA system that dominated the year's live shows – was stretching their resources well beyond endurable limits. They were forced to play bigger and bigger halls which, though financially attractive, was much less so musically and before things got too out of hand, Grateful Dead decided to take a break from performing.

It was an odd choice, considering that three-quarters of their income came from live gigs, but, as Garcia explained at the time, 'We're sort of up against the back end of success. We've unconsciously come to the end of what you can do in America, how far you can succeed, and it's nothing, it's nowhere. It means billions of cops and people busted at your gigs. It means high prices and hassling over extra-musical stuff. It's unnecessary so we're busting it. That's all. That's it.'

The break from performing (after a week at San Francisco's Winterland in October 1974, Grateful Dead did only four shows in the next 18 months) gave band members the chance to think for the first time in ages, and the chance to work on various solo projects. Garcia immersed himself in editing the hours of film shot at their 'farewell' concert, and worked on two more 'solo' projects: the romping live bluegrass album *Old and in the Way* and the quasi-Dead LP *Reflections*. Bobby Weir rocked out in Bay Area bars with the band Kingfish; Phil Lesh got weird with his friend Ned Lagin, putting out a sample of their forays into electronic music on *Seastones* (now a real collector's item, with copies going for $100 a shot); while Mickey Hart, who'd rejoined the band at their last gig, worked out with the Diga Rhythm Band.

Blues for Allah was the big band project of 1975. Released in September after some nine months work – twice as much as their previous two records combined – it marked a definite move toward more involved, almost jazz-like arrangement. Largely recorded at Weir's home studio, it's the most precisely resolved Grateful Dead album, and also marks Keith Godchaux' best effort with the band. He is literally all over the record, on organ here, electric piano there, from the rolling *Franklin's Tower* through the Santana-like jam on *Stronger than Dirt*, then on to the bounding reggae of *Crazy Fingers*. Another standout tune is Weir and Barlow's guided tour through the Grateful Dead universe, *The Music Never Stopped*.

They're a band beyond description,
like Jehovah's favorite choir
People joining hand in hand,
while the music plays the band,
Lord, they're setting us on fire.

Crazy rooster crowin' midnight,
balls of lightning roll along,
Old men sing about their dreams,
women laugh and children scream,
and the band keeps playing on.

Though the band hit the road again in the middle of 1976, their record company – the flagship of their quixotic quest for independence – was on its last legs. They'd already sold all the distribution rights to United Artists Records, and the last Grateful Dead album to come out on Grateful Dead Records, the two-record *Steal Your Face*, was released in June. Not even the brilliant Skull and Thunderbolt emblem on the cover could hide the disappointing live workout inside. No one in the band liked it, but they owed UA a record. One critic, the explosive Lester Bangs, had this response: 'Steal Your Face, Hah! Steal Your Money is more like it!' At least now, with all their contractual obligations fulfilled, they could start all over again.

After being courted by most of the majors, Grateful Dead decided to sign up with the new and relatively small label Arista, which had just been set up by ex-Columbia Records honcho Clive Davis. In exchange for a big advance to ease their financial worries, and equally much just to try something different, the band agreed to work with an outside producer for the first time in ten years. The August result, *Terrapin Station*, was their fastest seller since *Europe '72* five years before, thanks in large part to a massive 'A New Dead Era is Upon Us' promotional campaign.

The album itself is full of contrasts, with the opening side's poppy 'hits' – like Weir's *Estimated Prophet* and a cover of Marvin Gaye's *Dancin' in the Streets* – backed by the ambitious, side-long title suite, the lyrics of which come as close to self-explanation as Grateful Dead ever have on vinyl. But, to both the band and their fans, it was far from an unqualified success. After recording the tracks the band went on tour, leaving producer Keith Olsen, the man who made Fleetwood Mac's million-selling *Rumours*, to tidy things up and master the disc. When they came back they couldn't believe what he'd done, adding lush orchestrations, string quartets, even what sounds like the Mormon Tabernacle Choir, to make the Dead sound like he thought they should.

The best thing that happened in 1977 was the release, after some 1500 hours spent in the editing room, of the long-awaited 'Grateful Dead Movie', which was an immediate hit with the band and fans alike. 'The Village Voice' said of it, 'in 50 years when people want to know what a rock concert was like, they'll refer to this movie.' Garcia and soundman Dan Healy spent years getting the mix of sound and picture just right, and their efforts were well worthwhile. For instance, any time a band member is shown in close-up his part of the song is brought up on the soundtrack, so your ears zoom in along with the camera. Besides the in-concert footage, there's an in-depth look at the effort that went into transporting and setting up the 'Wall of Sound' PA, plus lots of hilarious interludes with dozy Deadheads waiting to get in to the show.

If any of the Grateful Dead were ever going to put out an album as slick as *Heaven Help the Fool*, Bob Weir would be the one, and he did. Weir hired producer Keith Olsen to do to him what he'd done to the Grateful Dead on *Terrapin*, and the resulting songs, released in January 1978, are undeniably catchy and listenable, with Bobby backed up by Waddy Wachtel, David Paich and Mike Porcaro, some of the hottest hands on the LA session circuit. In April Jerry Garcia followed suit with his fourth solo effort *Cats Under the Stars*, but the big event of this or any other year was the Dead's incredible trip to Egypt.

Playing at the pyramids was a dream come true for the band, though it didn't come to pass without some Herculean diplomatic efforts on their behalf. The idea had been rolling around in Dead circles since the late 1960s, but didn't get off the ground until Richard Loren, then the Dead's manager, returned from a scouting trip with proof that a suitable venue – the Gizeh Light and Sound Theatre, at the foot of the Great Pyramid – actually existed. In March of 1978, after the groundwork was laid by Joe Malone, a well-connected Washington DC expert in Middle Eastern affairs, Phil Lesh joined with Loren and the band's business manager Alan Trist to state their case to the Egyptian

Government. Phil, the band member who had 'wanted to go the baddest', explained that 'over the years we have played to many different people in many different places. We have learned that the context makes a difference. As musicians dedicated to live performance, this is a point of great interest to us, and we can think of no more inspiring a place to play than the Great Pyramid'. After that, they could hardly resist. As Alan Trist recalled, 'A smile bloomed on the Minister's face – he had understood!'

After a frantic few months spent getting all the necessary visas, permits and immunizations – and figuring out how to send 25 tons of the world's most sophisticated sound system, plus a hundred of the band's closest friends, halfway around the globe – all systems were go. Crew members arrived September 6, a week before the first show, to begin the arduous task of setting up the

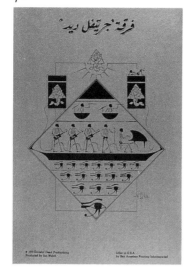

stage in the 110 degree heat, and the band trickled in over the next few days, along with Ken Kesey and a contingent of Pranksters, Bill Graham and even Bill Walton. Mickey arrived in time to celebrate his 35th birthday on September 11, and a hundred or so Deadheads flew in from San Francisco to join in the festivities. Although the primitive conditions made everything technical that much more difficult, the Manor Mobile recording truck was brought in from London in the hope of releasing a live record to help recoup the half-million dollars the adventure was costing.

Grateful Dead – Live at the Pyramids might have been a great title, but in the event the Dead didn't come up with good enough tracks to warrant an album. Not that that's why they came; as Garcia told *Melody Maker* at the time 'it doesn't matter if we play horribly, if everything breaks up – all the things that can go wrong from an aesthetic point of view to a technological point of view – all those things would be OK here.' Anyway, the whole thing was 'kind of like giving ourselves a present'. Besides being the experience of a lifetime, the gigs also raised some $20,000,

Adrian Boot

Adrian Boot

which went to support archaeological studies and to build soccer fields for local schoolkids. The band and entourage stayed on for another two weeks after the shows, visiting the temples of Karnak and Luxor and touring the Nile Valley. Mickey Hart found time to record native musicians in Sudan. These recordings were later released on Rykodisc as *Music From Upper And Lower Egypt*, the first in his *World Series*.

After the Pyramid Prank the Grateful Dead returned to California to put the finishing touches onto their next album, the first one they'd recorded at their own Le Club Front studio: *Shakedown Street*, produced by Little Feat guitar wizard Lowell George. Though on paper the match seemed made in heaven, in reality it was anything but ideal. For starters, though George was an ace guitar player he wasn't a producer, and had never produced a record before. He might have added his brilliant slide guitar as a musician, but didn't, and as a producer he was worse than useless. Although the songs – *Shakedown Street*, *Fire on the Mountain* and *I Need a Miracle* – were excellent, the resulting disc sounds fairly anemic and dissolute, despite the efforts of soundman Dan Healy (credited as co-producer) and John Kahn (associate producer). Deadheads feared the worst, at least until the band returned to form to close down Winterland with one of their all-time greatest shows.

It was probably because they could still reach such high points, albeit irregularly, that the Grateful Dead put off dealing with their underlying problems, mainly that Keith and Donna were less and less able to keep up with the band. Though the duo had contributed greatly to the band's output during the 70s, it was becoming increasingly obvious that they no longer fit in. For a start, Donna didn't play an instrument and looked distinctly uncomfortable onstage, so much so that whenever she wasn't needed to add a vocal she retired backstage. More worrying was Keith's attitude problem, largely drug-related, which showed up most obviously in his refusal to play anything but a concert grand piano onstage, at a time when the band was looking to broaden the range of their live sound.

So, early in 1979 the band made the decisive move of asking the Godchauxs if they'd mind quitting the band. In February the couple left amicably and the Dead, surprisingly quickly, found the perfect replacement: Brent Mydland, a soft-spoken Herbie Hancock fan who, like Keith, came from the unremarkable East Bay suburban town of Concord, California. After a briefly

successful attempt to break into the LA music business with a Top 40-type band named Silver – whose manager told him 'You can either rehearse and get really tight like Crosby, Stills and Nash, or you can fuck around and end up sounding like the Grateful Dead' – he moved back to the Bay Area and, ironically, got a job playing in Bob Weir's solo band. Two months later Bobby asked if he'd like to come and play with the Grateful Dead. He did, and after a couple of rehearsals played his first concert on April 22 at San Jose State's Spartan Stadium. 'I asked what tunes we were going to play, but no one would tell me. When we got on stage, I realized that *nobody* knew what we were going to play ...!' Welcome to the Grateful Dead, my friend. Brent's lively onstage demeanor, his flexibility as a keyboard player and his fine harmonies won the large crowd over immediately, and he has been a major part of the band's huge success in the 1980s.

Jay Blakesburg

Brent Mydland joins the band, April 22, 1979

Here's to 15 years of the Grateful Dead!

Jim Marshall

A year and a week after Brent's first show, Grateful Dead released their most energetic album in ages, *Go to Heaven*. From the opening notes of the opening tune – *Alabama Getaway*, which the Dead premiered on TV's 'Saturday Night Live' – you knew they'd found their feet again. With an irresistible riff and a turbocharged backbeat, it might have been a smash hit, though its crossover appeal was probably limited by Hunter's weird lyrics. Try to imagine some truckdriver cruising down the highway, singing along to lines like '23rd Psalm Major Domo, reserve me a table for two, down in the valley of the shadow, just me Alabama and you'. Another standout was the lilting *Althea*, and the whole band is in top form for a rousing version of *Don't Ease Me In*, the traditional favorite that, fifteen years before when they were still the Warlocks, was the band's first ever recording.

Although the Grateful Dead's 15th Anniversary was counted from June 7, 1965 – the day Phil moved to Palo Alto to join the Warlocks – the celebratory Folsom Field concerts proved to be only the beginning of festivities which lasted the rest of the year. The U.S. media rediscovered the Grateful Dead for the first time since the Summer of Love and repeatedly pegged the band as hippie holdouts. All sorts of features, both in print and on TV, repeated comparisons with the 1960s. The band, in turn, pointed out that many of their fans were 15 to 18-year-olds, just like at any rock concert. 'You look at the faces of 16-year-olds,' said Garcia, 'and you know they're not there for nostalgia. Check the crowd out. They're their own people.'

The highlight of the extended birthday party was, without a doubt, a series of concerts the Dead put together for their faithful at the Warfield Theater, an intimate, club-size hall in downtown San Francisco. Doing fifteen shows in just over two weeks, the Grateful Dead brought back the opening acoustic set they had introduced ten years before, which allowed them the chance to play many of the songs – *To Lay Me Down, Dire Wolf, Bird Song,* and especially *Ripple* – that hadn't survived the band's move into ever larger venues. The 15th Anniversary revue also played two nights in New Orleans before finishing off with a week of shows at New York's Radio City Music Hall.

Fortunately for those who weren't able to attend the shows in person, these special events were saved for posterity by recording masters Dan Healy and Betty Cantor-Jackson. The first batch was released the following spring as *Reckoning,* an all-acoustic two record selection that captures the subtle interaction between the musicians, and proves that even the bare bones version of the Grateful Dead is an absolutely unique musical enterprise. An electrified version, called *Dead Set,* was released in the fall, but isn't nearly as convincing, especially since many Deadheads had attended every show of the run and knew what the band had cooked up. What no one knew was that these proved to be the last of the band's vinyl output for the next six years.

It wasn't as if they'd lost their drive, for the Grateful Dead kept on playing some 75 concerts a year throughout the early 1980s. And they certainly hadn't lost their sense of humor: Grateful Dead celebrated Garcia's 40th birthday by playing a show at the Oklahoma City Zoo, and later did a night under the bright lights of the Aladdin Casino in Las Vegas.

Jerry and Bob even went on national TV, playing a few tunes – *Deep Elem Blues* and *The Monkey and The Engineer* – and shooting the breeze with David Letterman.

But it wasn't all fun and games around the Dead camp. In 1984 they finally got around to establishing a legal structure – the Rex Foundation, named after Donald 'Rex' Jackson, crew member and sometime road manager who died in 1978 – that could channel funds to all the good causes the band had become involved with over the years. In addition to their tradition of playing free concerts the band has always felt a social commitment, a desire to give something back to society as thanks for their good luck in being able to play music.

In fact, their first performance as the 'Grateful Dead' was a benefit for the San Francisco Mime Troupe, a radical street theater group, and throughout their career the band has continued to do benefit shows to help out their favorite anti-war, Native American, ecological and human service projects.

Another sign of the band's increasingly mature structure was their taking far greater control than ever before over the ticket selling arrangements for their concerts. The ad-hoc Deadhead grapevine which used to spread the word about impending shows was reinforced by a hotline number with the latest tour information, and Grateful Dead began selling 'tour booklets', containing an excellent ticket to every show in a given tour.

Still, how do you explain their going so many years without a new album? Maybe they just got tired of writing the necessary new songs. Garcia for one wouldn't disagree, for, as he said recently, 'I hate writing songs. I almost never write a song for

John Werner

fun. I'm not good at it, and I don't enjoy it. I'd rather do anything than write a song. Watch the grass grow, anything . . . and getting a new song out of Weir is like getting blood from a stone.' In fact, it couldn't have been too bad, because the band had already introduced a number of new songs – *West L.A. Fadeaway, Throwing Stones, Touch of Grey* – all of which were well established in the live set by the time the band's 20th Anniversary rolled around in 1985. The Dead celebrated with a weekend of shows at Berkeley's Greek Theatre, followed by a nationwide tour that was highlighted by multi-image slide shows recalling the band's exploits over the years.

Then, in July 1986, after a pair of shows in Washington D.C. with Bob Dylan and Tom Petty and the Heartbreakers, the unthinkable happened. Jerry Garcia fell ill and lapsed into a diabetic coma, and doctors rated his chances at slim going on zero. Much to his doctor's astonishment Jerry pulled through, though he virtually had to re-learn the guitar from scratch. 'I had to re-learn everything. Walking, talking, everything. It was like everything in my mind had gone into random access, into a big pot,' he told 'Q' Magazine. 'After a while I found that I could play the guitar again but I didn't know what I was playing. It was weird.'

All was back to normal in time for the New Year's shows, and a recharged Grateful Dead took over Veteran's Hall at the Marin County Civic Center and came out with what proved to be their most successful record ever – *In the Dark*. The album kicks off with the band's first ever Top Ten single, *Touch of Grey*, a somewhat wry look at getting older which features a locomotive rhythm, a catchy hook and an anthemic singalong refrain: *We will get by, we will survive*. Following hard on its heels is Weir, Brent and Barlow's roaring *Hell in a Bucket*, and the whole album, almost all of which was recorded in a live situation (albeit without an audience), fairly throbs with life.

The album's mass success caught Grateful Dead off their guard. 'Until *In the Dark* came out we were still pretty much underground, at least by our standards,' Weir told a 'Rockline' radio audience last year. 'We'd made some conscious efforts to achieve greater popularity ("We did those in 1966, but nobody seemed to notice," added Garcia) but we failed inutterably. After a while we just gave up on any notion of that and then we had a hit single, and people started noticing us. It surprised us a little.' Anticipating their 25th Anniversary, at the end of 1989 the band put out their tongue-in-cheekily titled follow-up LP *Built to Last*, complete with 'House of Cards' cover. After the runaway success of the almost live *In the Dark*, on the new album Grateful Dead adopted a completely different approach to recording. The basic rhythm tracks were recorded at George Lucas' Skywalker Ranch in northern Marin County, and the band members then evolved their individual parts on their own, interacting directly with the music even when they were all in separate rooms. Digital technology allowed slave copies to be made and worked on without any loss of sound quality, so the players could change their parts without muddying up the final mix. The end result is the cleanest sounding Grateful Dead record ever.

From the opening track, the *Foolish Heart* single, it's clear that Grateful Dead are not content to sit back and rest on their laurels. Musically the band is in top form, the drums exploding

behind chiming guitars and Brent's expanding pallet of keyboard textures. More than ever before the song lyrics – from Weir's *Victim or the Crime* (which he insists should have been the album title) to Brent and Barlow's *We Can Run, But We Can't Hide* – directly address the vital, real-world concerns of the 1990s, notably personal and planetary survival. Grateful Dead even venture into the imbroglio of world politics on *Standing on the Moon*, the side one closer that's proved to be a moving live epic:

> **There's a metal flag beside me, someone planted long ago**
> **Old Glory standing stiffly, crimson white and indigo**
> **I see all of Southeast Asia, I can see El Salvador**
> **I can hear the cries of children and the other songs of war**
> **It's like a mighty melody, that rings down from the sky**
> **Standing here, upon the moon, I watch it all roll by**

So what do the green and glasnostic 1990s hold in store for the Grateful Dead? A live album is in the works, as is a CD release of the best of the '*Space Jam*' segments. Then what? The Grateful Dead live from the Berlin Wall – or from the Space Shuttle – who can say? But is there an end in sight? 'Fuck no,' says Garcia. 'We're gonna keep on playing as long as we stay healthy ... until they drag us away ...'

David Letterman: What does it mean exactly ... the Deadheads? Is it just a catchy phrase or ...?

Garcia: Well, it just sort of turned up really ...

Weir: Well, there were acidheads, and there were speedheads, and grassheads, and now it turned into Deadheads

Letterman: Is that generally thought of as a flattering term?

Garcia: We think so

Weir: If the head fits, wear it

Deadhead tapers have recorded every show since the late 1960s

Bill Smythe

Bill Smythe

Bill Smythe

FAMILY DEAD

If there's one thing about the Grateful Dead that almost everybody would agree with, it's that there's nothing in the pop music world remotely like the relationship the band has with their fans – the Deadheads. Since the very beginning the audience has played a dynamic if indefinable role in the band's achievement, not only in supporting the band, financially and otherwise, but also in sustaining and energizing the spirit of adventure that still pervades most everything Grateful Dead.

It's missing the point to try to describe a 'typical' Grateful Dead fan, because if there's one thing they have in common it's that they're anything but typical. All sorts of folk like the good ol' Grateful Dead, for all sorts of reasons, but wherever they come from, and whatever they do in the 'real world', once the crowd gets together for a show there's an undeniable spirit of camaraderie that welcomes others of all shapes, sizes and states

Bill Smythe

Bill Smythe

'Following the Grateful Dead on tour is like running away and joining the circus. It's one of the last great adventures you can jump aboard as part of the American experience.'

Jerry Garcia

'Sometimes I feel like Richard Dreyfus' character in Close Encounters of the Third Kind. Sitting with his family at dinner one night, the memory of his alien sighting still weighing heavily on him, he stares into a pile of mashed potatoes sitting on his plate - he can't explain why - and whispers under his breath, *"This means something, this is important"*. And we learn that it is important. So is the Grateful Dead. The question remains, though - are they the aliens, or just the mashed potatoes...?'

Blair Jackson, The Golden Road

of mind. As lyricist John Barlow explained to David Gans, 'The community aspect is of major importance. Everybody says hello, does little *patois* things with each other ... they're a lot happier with the floating community of Deadheads than the average American is with the society he has with his fellow man. Communities used to be founded on geographic or economic bases. This one is based on something vaguely spiritual, and it has no geographical location – but it is just as much a community as any mining town.'

Jay Blakesburg

Grateful Dead is a lot more than the six musicians you see on stage, and the band would be the first to admit that they couldn't make it through a show, much less 25 years of shows, without the help of the dozens of people who work behind the scenes. Most of this extended 'family' have been around from the start, and over the years the same people have taken on a variety of roles and jobs within the loosely structured, mob-rule democracy of the Grateful Dead organisation, Kidd Candelario, for example, who's responsible for keeping Phil's equipment working happily,

Kidd and Parish sabotage Jerry's guitar

Grateful Dead hotline:

(201) 777-8653 East Coast

(415) 457-6388 West Coast

Ticket information: (415) 457-8457

Sound wizard Dan Healy with Ultra Sound's

Don Pearson and Howard Danchik

is also the head of Grateful Dead's merchandising wing, while Danny Rifkin, who co-managed the band for much of their career, now looks after the affairs of the Rex Foundation, a registered charity for whom the band does annual benefit concerts. Others are more actively involved with the actual performances, like soundman Dan Healy, who virtually invented the Dead's unsurpassed sound system, and lighting magician Candace Brightman, who somehow finds just the right light to suit the ever-changing musical mood.

DEAD LIVE...

Almost everything about the Grateful Dead – from their essentially improvisational approach to making music, to the dynamic interactions of their audience – can be traced back to the Acid Tests. For all their importance, the first half-dozen Acid Tests were fairly small affairs, usually involving around 300 people, including the fifty or so performers. The Trips Festival, held at San Francisco's Longshoreman's Hall in January 1966, brought everything to a higher level, garnering media attention and showing would-be promoters that there was an audience for, and money to be made from, the new music. It also convinced those involved that the Acid Tests were about to take over the world. As Phil Lesh remembers, 'When the first Trips Festival happened, to realize that there were fully 5000 people in the San Francisco Bay Area alone who were on the same trip as we were – because there they were, all dancing at the same time: we'd go 'brangh-nangh-nangh', and they were all dancing, up and down in waves – was truly one of the most exciting things one could imagine. If there's *this* many of us, how many more are there out there, waiting to become this ... We Are Everywhere ... It was the best news we'd ever heard in our lives, and it still is. You can get together and have a good time, and you don't have to be afraid of anybody.'

'We became Grateful Dead at the Acid Tests'

Phil Lesh

Jim Marshall

Jim Marshall

The spirit of adventure and discovery that motivated the Acid Tests carried over into the band's live shows, many of which they set up at church meeting halls, college gyms and other unusual locations. While down in LA with the Prankster crew – minus Kesey, who was hiding out in Mexico – Grateful Dead did a couple of gigs on their own, including one at Troupers Hall. As Rosie McGee remembers, 'Troupers Hall was the meeting room for a retired actors' club in Hollywood. The rent for the gig couldn't have been much. We did everything ourselves, all in two days. We plastered handbills all over Hollywood. Stage decor was a few lengths of paisley cloth purchased that afternoon at a fabric store. For a box office, we had a card table and a cigar box. Our not-quite-full house must have had over a hundred people, and when the night was over our net take was $75. At 2 o'clock in the morning we went to Cantor's Deli on Fairfax and spent it on dinner for everybody – with dessert.'

'We played extended pieces from the beginning. We just never thought of stopping; it never crossed our minds to play three minute songs.'

Bill Kreutzmann

Grateful Dead in Hollywood, March 25 1966

Rosie McGee Ende

Jim Marshall

Grateful Dead

Before the Fillmore and Avalon scenes got going, the Grateful Dead were doing regular gigs at the Matrix, a small club run by Marty Balin of Jefferson Airplane. It's from a gig here on January 7, 1966 that the earliest set list survives to tell future generations the sort of tunes the Dead were doing. Starting off with *It's a Sin*, which survived in the repertoire until the '70s, Grateful Dead went on to cover *On the Road Again*, Dylan's *She Belongs to Me* and *Baby Blue*, as well as R 'n' B classics like Wilson Pickett's *Midnight Hour*.

Gene Anthony

Bobby and Phil in rehearsal at the Sausalito Heliport

Gene Anthony

At the end of the summer Grateful Dead played free outdoor
concerts in Golden Gate Park, hiring a flatbed truck and a
generator and setting up in the sun. Though most of these were
spur-of-the-moment affairs, a few were planned and publicised
well in advance, sometimes to raise money for a good cause, other
times to make a political point. On October 6, 1966, Grateful
Dead played at what was billed as the 'Lunatic Protest
Demonstration' to mark the criminalization of LSD, which up
until then had been a controlled but legal substance.

One of the many distinctive aspects of Grateful Dead's concerts
were the magnificent posters used to advertise them. Graphic
artists Alton Kelly and Stanley Mouse worked together on what
immediately became one of the Dead's most identifiable images,
the 'Skull and Roses', first used for the band's September 16, 1966
gig at the Family Dog's Avalon Ballroom. The posters were so
popular that they were soon being given away with each ticket
purchased.

**Lunatic Protest Demonstration in the Panhandle,
Golden Gate Park.**

Gene Anthony

Grateful Dead at the Human Be-in, sharing the stage with poet Lenore Kandel and political activist Jerry Rubin

The tribal stomp January 14, 1967 in Golden Gate Park, where the Dead played with Jefferson Airplane, Big Brother and the Holding Company, the Charlatans, Quicksilver Messenger Service and Country Joe and the Fish, was for many the peak experience of the early days of the Haight. A makeshift festival, promoted as 'A Gathering of Tribes for the first Human Be-in' by the Haight-based 'Oracle' newspaper, it surprised everyone involved by attracting some 20,000 people – five times more than had ever made the scene before – to the Polo Fields in Golden Gate Park for a Saturday in the sun. Gary Snyder, Timothy Leary and dozens more also joined in the fun, and Allen Ginsburg ended the afternoon by leading the crowd in a Buddhist chant.

While the Summer of Love was turning the Haight Ashbury into a media circus, Grateful Dead spent most of the time on tour. The main event for the band happened at The Straight Theatre on Haight Street on September 29th, when Mickey Hart joined the band for a two hour jam on *Alligator* – and stayed for most of the next twenty-odd years. By the next year things had calmed down enough that the city agreed to close Haight Street and let the Grateful Dead do a free Sunday afternoon concert.

Mike Polillo

Jim Marshall

Mickey Hart on Haight Street, March 3, 1968

Jim Marshall

Jim Marshall

Rosie McGee Ende

In May 1968, after playing a surprise show at Columbia University in support of the student strike, Grateful Dead played a free concert Sunday afternoon in Central Park

'The 1960s as we experienced them had a lot of intelligence and good humor, but what it was about for us was fun. It was about almost nothing but that, and I mean fun with a capital F. I mean real fun, the kind of fun that takes your imagination, and is as fun as you could hope for fun to be.'

Jerry Garcia

(OPPOSITE) Pigpen, Jerry and Phil at the Newport Pop Festival, August 1968

Jim Marshall

After a summer of shows on the West Coast, Grateful Dead did a quick tour of the Midwest, during which they played with Procul Harum and Blood Sweat and Tears. Starting with a concert November 23 they were joined by keyboard player Tom Constanten, an old music school chum of Phil's who'd been helping out in the studio while the Dead were working on *Aoxomoxoa*. Both in the studio and playing live, 'TC' added a whole new spectrum to the Grateful Dead sound – playing prepared piano ala John Cage and contributing a range of bizarre effects – especially on extended plunges through *Dark Star* and the like. The band returned to San Francisco for an all-night New Years' gig at Winterland (9pm to 9am including breakfast) with Santana and QMS.

Tom Constanten joins Grateful Dead,

New Year's Eve, 1968/9

Sky River Music Festival outside Seattle in

September 1968

Grateful Dead play Woodstock

'We tried to play our little music in the midst of this incredible confusion. For some reason or another we didn't trust the PA they had there that everybody else was using. So there was this long delay, maybe four or five hours, interminable. When you multiply that by the number of people at Woodstock you get several human years . . .

'We went out on the stage, which was packed with people. It was getting to be very, um, *wired* out there . . . everything was conductive in some weird way. It looked like there were balls of electricity bouncing across the stage and jumping on my guitar. The lights were superhot, giganto spotlights, so there was this kind of bug-on-a-microscope sensation, of being pinned by these spotlights – and knowing there were 300,000 people out there but not being able to see *anybody* because of the darkness and the blinding light. It was nightmarish beyond belief.'

Jerry Garcia on Woodstock

Despite their miserable performance at Woodstock, for the next two years the Dead were virtually transplanted to New York, playing more shows there than they did anywhere else. Their main base of operations was Bill Graham's newly opened NYC branch. This new venue, which he christened the Fillmore East, was to see some of the best shows the Dead have ever done. At some of these shows they shared the bill with the Allman Brothers Band, which proved to be an excellent musical pairing, since both groups had two relentless drummers, a pair of ace guitarists, and a love of improvisational playing.

In 1969 GD played more concerts in more places than ever before, as this brief list shows:

Feb 7 Pittsburgh, PA. Two shows with the Velvet Underground.

March 21 Rose Palace, Pasadena with Jethro Tull

April 5 Avalon Ballroom with Flying Burrito Brothers

May 28 People's Park Bail Ball benefit with Creedence Clearwater Revival, Santana and Jefferson Airplane

June 22 Central Park New York City

Aug 16 Woodstock

Sept 1 New Orleans Pop Fest

Dec 13 San Bernardino, Swing Auditorium

Dec 28 Hollywood Pop Fest Hollywood Florida

Dec 31 New Year's Eve Boston Tea Party

Grateful Dead

Another of the many memorable double bills around this time was a weekend of concerts the Grateful Dead played at the Fillmore West in April 1970, which were opened by the Miles Davis Quintet. Phil remembers it as 'cold-blooded murder' having to follow him, but as Kreutzmann recalls, 'We played really fast and loose, because I couldn't get Miles out of my head. It had a tremendous effect on what we played that night.'

'By the late 1960s we were on the road a lot, so we were no longer part of a stable local community. We were nomads, traveling around America, and at that time lots of parts of America had never experienced anything strange at all. We were the first weird people a lot of those places ever saw.'

Jerry Garcia

The first year of the new decade found Grateful Dead running in overdrive, touring almost constantly – 145 shows in 22 states and three countries – most of which were presented as 'An Evening with the Grateful Dead featuring the New Riders of the Purple Sage'. The New Riders were a natural outgrowth of the band's move into simpler, more 'countrified' music, and featured guitar-playing, jug-band friends David Nelson and John 'Marmaduke' Dawson, who co-wrote *Friend of the Devil*. Initially supported by Garcia on pedal steel, Lesh on bass and Mickey on drums, NRPS evolved into an independent group but continued to be a part of the extended Grateful Dead musical family.

(opposite) May 1970 brought them to England for the first time, playing the Hollywood Festival at Newcastle-under-Lyme with Traffic, Jose Feliciano and Black Sabbath

TOUR DATES EUROPE '72

April 7, 8 Empire Pool, Wembley

April 11 City Hall, Newcastle

April 14 Tivoli Theatre, Copenhagen

April 16 Arhus University, Denmark

April 17 Tivoli Gardens, Copenhagen

April 21 Beat Club, Bremen, W. Germany

April 24 Reinhalle, Dusseldorf, W. Germany

April 26 Jahrhundert Halle, Frankfurt, W. Germany

April 29 Musikhalle, Hamburg, W. Germany

May 3, 4 Olympia Theatre, Paris

May 7 Bickershaw Festival, Manchester

May 10 Concertgebouw, Amsterdam

May 11 Civic Hall, Rotterdam

May 13 Fairgrounds, Lille, France

May 16 Radio Luxembourg (Live radio broadcast)

May 18 Deutsches Museum Halle, Munich, W. Germany

May 23–26 The Strand Lyceum, London

November : EUROPE '72 Album released

'Europe '72 was the answer to a whole lot of questions, like how the hell are we gonna be able to take the entire staff and crew on a European vacation ... lo and behold, the album actually paid for the tour, which I thought was a nice way to do it.'

Bob Weir

Mary Ann Mayer

Mary Ann Mayer

In June Grateful Dead returned to the States, playing a show at the Hollywood Bowl on June 17 that, sadly, proved to be Pigpen's last appearance on stage. For the next nine months his health, eroded by years of heavy drinking, gradually worsened. He died, aged 27, on March 8, 1973.

Though in the early days Pigpen was the best musician of the bunch, and the only one willing to play frontman for the band, he was always something of an anomaly in the Grateful Dead, preferring whisky and the blues to psychedelics and space. In contrast to his prowling stage demeanor, in person he was quiet and introverted. Mickey Hart has said, 'He had to look tough, because he was so gentle that he'd get stepped on.' Despite his rough-looking exterior it was Pigpen who introduced the whole 'love each other' trip, urging people at shows to turn around and say hello to the people next to them, shake their hands, get to know one another. 'If I could have one wish in the world,' says Phil, 'it would be that Pigpen could still be with us.'

Ronald C. McKernan

1945–1973

Pigpen was

and is now forever

one of the

Grateful Dead

'I really liked that son-of-a-bitch - he had a lot of love in his heart. He was a guy who was jokingly mean...He had a motorcycle jacket that was a little scary; he had that look. He was unkempt, to say the least. But he was the leader of the band.'

Bill Kreutzmann

Grateful Dead spent most of 1973 on the road, hauling around the massive PA system that evolved into the 'Wall of Sound' and playing shows in 26 of the lower 48 states, including what still stands as the biggest rock concert ever, the July 28 'Summer Jam' concert at Watkins Glen racetrack in Upstate NY. Along with the Allman Brothers and the Band, Grateful Dead played for a crowd of 600,000, and set up digitally delayed speaker towers so that everyone could hear clearly. They also added an extra set of amplifiers (fortunately the factory was just down the road), and broadcast the show live over the radio to the estimated million other fans who were stuck in the massive traffic snarl up on the way to the site. Good ol' Grateful Dead . . .

Jerry and friends play at Santa Barbara,

May 1973

Richard Pechner

Richard Pechner

(ABOVE) Vancouver 1974. Notice the double microphones, which were supposed to minimize background noise and feedback by cancelling out any sound that went through both

(LEFT) Setting up the Wall of Sound, Reno 1974

(BELOW) Wall of Sound at the Hollywood Bowl, August 1974

Richard Pechner

Mary Ann Mayer

The 'Wall of Sound' was developed over many years as part of Grateful Dead's ongoing effort to have the best possible concert sound. By the early 1970s the band found themselves playing to ever greater numbers of people, and to overcome the lousy sound that so often accompanied the cavernous venues, Grateful Dead, through their lifelong soundman Dan Healy, invested lots of time and money trying out various ideas and theories in search of acoustic nirvana.

The end result of many years' work was unveiled at San Francisco's Cow Palace in March 1974, and consisted of some 600 speakers wired up in eleven distinct channels, with the whole thing charged by four dozen McIntosh 2300 power amps cranking out over 26,000 watts RMS. The most unusual aspect of the system, besides its impressive bulk, was that each musician had his own sonically independent system, so no two sounds went through the same speaker, which effectively wiped out any distortion. Also, the whole 50-foot-high rig was set up behind the players, removing the need for a separate monitor system and giving the band a clear idea of what was going out to the audience.

Mary Ann Mayer

Needless to say, it was loud, and when it worked it was, as Dan Healy says, 'truly a kick in the ass'. However, it took so long to set up and get right, and was such a bear to haul around, that within a few months the Wall was burning everybody out. Combined with many other pressures that Grateful Dead were under, by the end of the year they called it quits, retired the Wall and went fishing.

Bringing the sonic quest up to date, the Dead's current PA system builds on the 'Wall of Sound' experience but is generally much more reliable. It still puts out the best sound around, but with far fewer headaches for the crew. The fully computerized 1990 PA is roughly five times more efficient than earlier set-ups, and is pressing at the boundaries of theoretical acoustic perfection. 50,000 watts RMS pump out a potent 105 dB of crystal clear sound, and that's only turned up halfway! For larger stadium shows, the normal 900 speakers, including an 8 foot block of 18″ bass speakers, are supplemented by digitally-delayed speaker towers that extend out into the audience, so no one misses out on the fun.

One of the biggest boons of the computer age is that Healy and co. can now use CAD programs to plot out the perfect speaker alignment for any venue that Grateful Dead might play, feeding in the floor plan and manipulating the PA configuration on the screen until everything is just right. It's much easier than shifting 50 tons of sound equipment hoping to hit on the right solution, and has meant that unintentional echoes have been completely silenced. It also means that the PA set-up looks completely different every place they play. Other developments have come about as a result of MIDI technology, which allows the players to send their signals through digital synthesizers to massively broaden the range of sounds and tones. It's also meant that it's now sometimes very hard to tell just who's playing what, even moreso since Healy can now take their sound, 'turn it upside down and then send it back to them' – something he does to great effect during the 'Space Jam' segments.

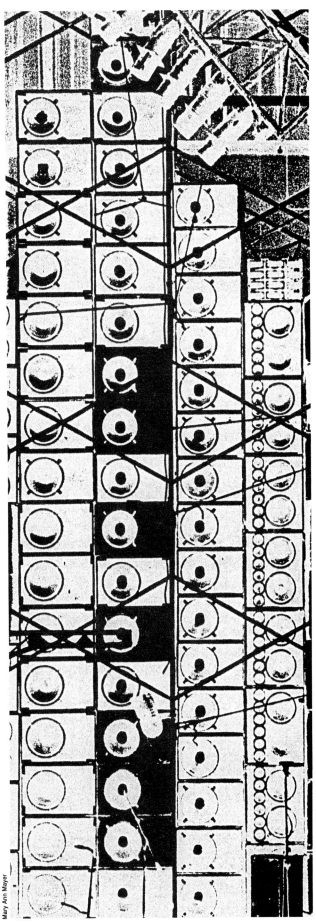

Mary Ann Mayer

After Grateful Dead retired the Wall of Sound PA system, they took an extended break for the next eighteen months, playing only four shows, all of them in San Francisco. The first was at the Students Need Athletics, Culture and Kicks (SNACK) Benefit at Kezar Stadium in March 1975, at which they shared the bill with the Doobie Brothers, Neil Young, Tower of Power and other Bay Area musicians. For their part of the show, joined by Ned Lagin and Merl Saunders, Grateful Dead played an extended jam from *Blues for Allah*, ending with a wild *Johnny B. Goode*. Six months later the band returned to the park, this time to celebrate their 10th Anniversary with a free concert for 50,000 fans in Lindley Meadows, joined by Jefferson Starship.

Jim Marshall

In June 1976 Grateful Dead hit the road again, touring the US before a week of shows (July 14–18) at the intimate Orpheum Theater in San Francisco. The big show of the year took place at the Oakland Coliseum in October, when the band joined with the Who at a weekend of 'Days on the Green'. The Dead opened the first day, and closed the second, after which the NME caught Pete Townsend telling Jerry Garcia, 'I've got to hand it you guys, you played five hours two nights running and didn't repeat a song. We've been playing the same set for six years.'

Richard Pechner

(ABOVE) Carlos Santana joins the Grateful Dead, New Year's 1976

Bruce Polonsky

BGP Archives

DEAD LIVE AT THE PYRAMIDS

Somewhat surprisingly, very few American fans joined in on the Pyramid Prank, though 100 or so made it on an all-in $999 package tour from San Francisco. All told, about 2000 people attended each of the shows, half of them Egyptians, including a number of robed Bedouin tribesmen who followed the music across the desert sands, hopped down off their camels and started dancing.

The concert program, printed in English and Arabic, stressed the band's musical pluralism, and said: 'Above all, the Grateful Dead are what they experience, and their music is most poignant at each new live musical encounter, and is there enriched. It is the quest for new musical experience that brings them to Egypt, where the timeless history of the Nile and the compelling enigma of the greatest of monuments, the Pyramids, have long inspired them with the dream of performing in a context of such cultural and historical depth.'

Richard Loren

'The idea behind going to play there was to hear how our music would sound in a radically different environment and to see the gut reaction of people who didn't know *Sugaree* and didn't know *Truckin'*; we wanted to move them with new music.'

Mickey Hart

The band tried to make things more accessible to the locals by having Sudanese tar player Hamza El-Din open the shows. On the first night his set blended into a 45 minute version of *Not Fade Away*; on the second night Grateful Dead started, then Hamza joined to kick off the second set. The third night, September 16, was the night when everything seemed to come together. Keith finally got a properly tuned piano, Weir's guitar problems were all solved, and to top it off, when the band took the stage the full Piscean moon was in eclipse. Paul Krassner knew it was going to be special when he heard Garcia, before he counted off the first song, *Bertha*, say to the band, 'Remember . . . play in tune.' The second set was opened by Hamza again, and ended in a rousing version of *Round and Around*, followed by the one and only encore of the stand, *One More Saturday Night*. As Bill Graham later said, 'The third night was one of the great experiences of my life – dancing to *Sugar Magnolia* in front of the Great Pyramid. In my old age, if I remember major events in my life, this will be one of them.'

The whole Egypt affair was a great success for all concerned. Though the recordings didn't prove exceptional enough to warrant an album, the adventure got enough press coverage to make Arista happy. The Egyptian ambassador to the U.S. put his official seal of approval on the event, in a letter to the Grateful Dead: 'The accounts in both the Egyptian and the American press give me, as they must give you and your colleagues, great satisfaction. It is a historic first in the annals of modern music – to play the Pyramids before thousands of fans, old and new. My sincere congratulations, and best wishes of success to the Grateful Dead.'

Bill Smythe

(ABOVE) Guitar maestro John Cippolina joins

Grateful Dead at La Fayette College, Pennsylvania,

to celebrate Billy's 33rd birthday

Grateful Dead returned to the US to put the final touches on their new album *Shakedown Street*, which they debuted on NBC's super-popular 'Saturday Night Live'. In making the show the band also made friends with John Belushi and Dan Ackroyd, who in their guise as the "Blues Brothers" helped the Dead ring in the New Year at Winterland. Rated as one of the all-time best Grateful Dead shows, it was also the last gig played there before the venue was demolished to make way for condos.

BGP Archives

Bill Graham rides in on a giant joint at the close of

Winterland, New Year's Eve 1978–79

The biggest change Grateful Dead made to get ready for the 1980s was to add keyboard wizard Brent Mydland to the lineup in place of Keith and Donna Godchaux. Though Brent came from a more conventional musical world than the one Grateful Dead inhabit, he had little trouble finding his way. As he has said, 'I like the looseness of this music, not feeling I have to do the same thing every time. Rehearsals take place on stage more than anywhere else. The tunes are worked up real loose, then it's like, "OK, that's pretty much how it goes. Let's leave it a little rough, that way we've got something to play with." '

(ABOVE) Brent Mydland at home behind the keyboards, Warfield 1980

Jay Blakesburg

Jerry, Billy and Bobby bring in the 1980s at the first of many New Year's shows at Henry J. Kaiser in Oakland

GRATEFUL DEAD'S 15th ANNIVERSARY YEAR – 1980

At one of the first concerts Grateful Dead did in 1980 – an April Fool's day concert at Capitol Theater in Passaic New Jersey – they kicked off with a version of Chuck Berry's *The Promised Land*, with the musicians all taking each other's instruments. Mickey Hart lead the way on vocal and rhythm guitar, Phil played lead guitar, Bobby keyboards, Billy on bass and Jerry and Brent on drums. After this they switched back to normal and started all over again . . .

Most of the hoopla that came to dominate this 15th Anniversary year started with the media, not with the band, who've never been all that keen on nostalgia. The Dead's own 'official' 15th Anniversary celebration was held June 7 & 8, 1980 – 15 years from the day Phil joined the band – at Folsom Field in Boulder Colorado.

The year's most special occasions took place in the fall, when Grateful Dead played a series of retrospective concerts September 25 to October 14 at the Warfield Theatre in San Francisco and October 22–30 at New York City's Radio City Music Hall, split by a two-night stand in New Orleans. All of the shows started off with an acoustic set, which enabled them to bring back many of the quieter songs that the Dead hadn't performed since the early 1970s.

Acoustic set at the Warfield, 1980

Jay Blakesburg

Bob Minkin

Bob Minkin

In 1981 Grateful Dead did two quick tours of Europe, their only shows there in the 1980s. Just for fun Jerry and Bobby did an all-acoustic show at a small club in Amsterdam, and when later shows planned for the South of France fell through at the last minute, the whole band came back to Amsterdam, borrowed what equipment they could and played two of their hottest shows, the second to celebrate Bobby's 34th birthday. Dubbed the 'Oops Concerts', the reigning chaos freed them up enough to bring back songs they hadn't played for years, notably Van Morrison's rocking *Gloria* and Pigpen's trademark *Lovelight*, which Phil described as 'like a great orgasm'.

A good humored 1982 was brought to a fitting close with what was by consensus one of the all-time great New Year's shows, especially since Robert Hunter made a rare appearance onstage kicking off the night's proceedings with the Dinosaurs. Another highlight was Bill Graham's traditional entrance dressed as Father Time, riding on a giant mushroom. There's been ongoing debate amongst Deadheads as to whether it was *P, strictipes* or the more potent *P. baeocystis,* but in either case it was the largest specimen ever encountered, and caused a definite intoxication in the 8000 revellers.

(OPPOSITE TOP) Fender bender at the Melk Weg, Amsterdam

(OPPOSITE BELOW) Close Encounters of the New Year's kind ... Bill Graham rides into 1982 on an unidentified high-flying object

(BOTTOM) Grateful Dead celebrate Garcia's 40th with an open-air concert in the Oklahoma City zoo

New Year 1982 – 3, Bill Graham rides a wild mushroom

Ken Friedman/BGP Archives

Bill Smythe

Just like Grandma Moses

Just like Auld Lang Syne

Play the change, however strange

And get it right this time

It's been a hard haul

20 as the crow flies,

When your back's to the wall

Got to play it as it lies

Come hear Uncle John's Band

Playing to the years

Come along or go alone

Like an avalanche or a rolling stone

Wave that flag !

Wave it while you can

Long as you keep coming

You got a band

Harmonizing convergence at Front Street, 1985

Rosie McGee Ende

Bill Smythe

Red Rocks 1985, complete with 75' PA towers

Ken Friedman

As shown by their trip to Egypt, the Dead have always been keen to play at unusual locations, at power spots charged with sympathetic magic. Red Rocks, an old WPA amphitheatre that the Dead more or less 'discovered' outside Denver, has long been a favorite, despite the variable weather and the difficult acoustics. They haven't always had to search for the magic, though. Sometimes it came looking for them, as at Portland in 1980, when the Mount St. Helens volcano erupted just as Grateful Dead broke into *Fire on the Mountain*.

(ABOVE) Golden Gate sunset at the Greek Theatre, Berkeley

Telluride 1987. In their effort to get away from the anonymous municipal stadia they find themselves having to play, Grateful Dead have begun doing summer concerts in the mountains, often at downhill ski areas like Park City or Mammoth Mountain

Ken Friedman/BGP Archives

The collaboration between Bob Dylan and the Grateful Dead was on the cards for a long time before it actually happened. The Dead have always admired his work and have sung many of his tunes in concert, but it wasn't until the summer of 1986 – during a joint tour on which Dylan was backed by Tom Petty and the Heartbreakers – that they got together on stage, if only for a couple of songs. During the next summer's stadium shows, billed as 'Alone and Together', the Dead did their standard two sets before being joined by the man himself for an extended journey through Dylan's entire back catalogue.

Ken Friedman

Though it was all done for the fun of it – Weir says they rehearsed over 100 songs, some even twice! – all the shows were recorded for posterity. From the hours of tape Garcia and engineer John Cutler culled *Dylan and the Dead*, a rough and ready album

reminiscent of Dylan's *Before the Flood* workout with The Band,
that features sterling versions of *Knocking on Heaven's Door* and
All Along the Watchtower.

'As long as I can breathe, and as long as we can play together and have fun, we'll grow old with the music and the music will grow old with us. There's no reason why we can't play till we drop. That'd by a good way of going – I'd rather do that than drop in front of a TV set drinking beer. Anyway, this music is medicine. It makes me young. It *feels* young, real good.'

Mickey Hart

'For those who are drawn into whatever it is we do, through whatever avenues or for whatever reasons, we can and do supply a little genuine joy. I don't know if that's a complete reason for being, either for me personally or for the band, but it's a good holding pattern until we find out if there's something more to go for.'

Bob Weir

'The Grateful Dead have proven that you *can* get there from here. It's just that there's no tickets available.'

Bill Kreutzmann

'Grateful Dead is the most open forum that any musician can have, next to playing in a great jazz band. I'm the lucky guy in rock and roll; I get to experiment, I get to improvise. I don't have to play the same tune every night. I don't have to play any tune the same way twice. To me, it's been gratifying beyond my wildest dreams to play in this band.'

Phil Lesh

'I know these guys better than I know anybody. And they still have that capacity to surprise me musically; I have to stay on my toes to keep up with them. At the same time, if I have an inspiration, they're all ears. They'll follow me down any dark alley. Sometimes there's light at the end of the alley, and sometimes there's a black hole. The point is, you don't get adventure in music unless you're willing to take chances.'

Jerry Garcia

'Tightness is not what the Dead stands for. If things are too planned out it can take away the interest. But I like the way we work. It's like doing jam sessions for a living.'

Brent Mydland

Bob Minkin

Suzanne Vega leads the Dead through 'Chinese Bones' at the Rainforest Benefit

Bob Minkin

Garcia and bluesman Mick Taylor get down on 'Little Red Rooster'

Grateful Dead and Clarence 'The Big Man' Clemons rock the Oakland Arena, raising $300,000 to aid victims of the San Francisco earthquake

At the Rainforest Benefit, which capped a record-breaking 9-night run at New York's Madison Square Garden in September 1988, Grateful Dead were joined by a galaxy of popstars including Hall & Oates and Bruce Hornsby and the Range. Besides the vital consciousness-raising, the event earned nearly half a million dollars for the Save the Rainforest campaign, something the entire band wholeheartedly supports. As Bob Weir explains, 'In ten years if we have not reversed what's going on now with the destruction of the Earth's biomass, then it will be irreversible, and protein life as we know it will no longer be able to happen.' Adds Garcia, 'So unless you're an insect, you might want to do something about it.'

For further information contact:

GREENPEACE
(USA):
1436 U Street NW,
Washington DC 20009.
(UK):
30-31 Islington Green,
London N1 8XE.

FRIENDS OF THE EARTH
(USA):
218 D Street SE,
Washington DC 20003.
(UK):
26-28 Underwood Street, London N1 7JU.

WORLD WIDE FUND FOR NATURE
(WORLD WILDLIFE FUND)
(USA):
1250 24th Street NW,
Washington DC 20037.
(UK):
Panda House,
Weyside Park,
Godalming,
Surrey GU7 1XR.

Susana Millman

" ... And we bid you goodnight"